IMAGES OF ENGLAND

# BRADFORD PUBS

IMAGES OF ENGLAND

# BRADFORD PUBS

PAUL JENNINGS

The
History
Press

*Frontispiece*: Mine hosts and staff outside the Black Swan in Thornton Road in the summer of 1915 or 1916. From left to right are: the barmaid, barman, waiter (who had an artificial leg), landlord Arthur Gray, landlady Sarah Gray and a neighbouring shopkeeper. Arthur had previously worked for a wine merchant and been head barman at the Grosvenor in Ivegate. Sarah was noted for her ability to handle rough customers and this part of Bradford must have had a fair few.

First published in 2004 by Tempus Publishing

Reprinted in 2009 by
The History Press
The Mill, Brimscombe Port,
Stroud, Gloucestershire, GL5 2QG
www.thehistorypress.co.uk

Reprinted 2012, 2013

British Library Cataloguing in Publication Data.
A catalogue record for this book is available from the British Library.

ISBN 978 0 7524 3302 8

Typesetting and origination by Tempus Publishing Limited.
Printed in Great Britain.

# Contents

# Acknowledgements

I either took or commissioned many of the photographs in this collection during my research into the history of Bradford's pubs. Several private individuals were kind enough to allow me to copy and use their photographs. I would like to thank the following for permission to use photographs: Bass North, Bradford Libraries, the Bradford Heritage Recording Unit, Bradford Housing and Environmental Health and Bradford Museums, Galleries and Heritage for the Crichton prints. I am also indebted to the work of Bradford Camera Club members, in particular that of the late Mrs M. Bruce, who photographed Bradford before so much of it disappeared and whose collection is kept at Bradford Central Library. Thanks too to William Sutherland for the sketch map and the redrawing of pub plans.

As to the historical information, I once again thank the staff of the various libraries and archive offices where I undertook my research. I would like to acknowledge the information on breweries provided by Malcolm Toft, plus information from many others whose brains I have picked at various times. Finally, I thank my wife, Felicity, for reading the text and I hope saving me from at least some of the grumpiness that too often finds its way into local history writing.

# Introduction

The images in this book cover the period from about 1870 through to the close of the twentieth century. I have examined the pubs within the perimeters of the original Bradford municipal borough of 1847, which was created from the amalgamation of four separate townships: Bowling, Bradford, Horton and Manningham. This covered a considerable area, the outer boundaries being Daisy Hill in the west, Laisterdyke in the east, Horton Bank Top in the south and Undercliffe in the north, all of which overlook the great natural bowl in which Bradford is situated. It contained a lot of pubs, the number peaking in 1869 when there were nearly 600; one for every 240 persons in the town. It is from these pubs in this area that the images are drawn, although the town went on to absorb a number of other neighbouring districts which constituted the city and county borough of Bradford.

What were the origins of those 600 pubs? In fact the term 'pub' only came into common use quite late in the nineteenth century and 'the pub' evolved from a variety of establishments. At the beginning of the nineteenth century, there was a hierarchy of drinking places. At the top were the coaching inns, from which the stage coaches departed and from where food and accommodation were provided for travellers. Coaching inns in Bradford were places such as the Bowling Green in Bridge Street, the Sun at the bottom of Ivegate, the Talbot in Kirkgate and the White Swan in Market Street. Next below them in the hierarchy were smaller inns or public houses. The term 'public house' dates back to the late seventeenth century. They offered a range of services. Some, for example, provided a base for carriers delivering goods to neighbouring towns and villages. Others were a convenient location to transact business on market days or when attending the Piece Halls for the sale of worsted cloth – hence the existence of several houses in Kirkgate, like the Shoulder of Mutton or the White Lion. Further down in the hierarchy were the more humble alehouses, although this term was already somewhat archaic by the nineteenth century. These alehouses could offer a venue for friendly society meetings but their essential function was as a social centre for drink, conversation, music and games – the essential pub pastimes then as now.

All three types of establishment required a licence from the magistrates; this was a requirement first introduced in as early as 1552. The records of those annual licensing or brewster sessions show that in 1803, there were fifty-seven licences held, a number which had risen to seventy-two by 1827. At this time, Bradford was experiencing rapid growth; principally due to its worsted trade, it was the fastest-growing industrial centre in the country. The population rose from 13,264 in 1801 to over 100,000 fifty years later.

As magistrates of the time were only willing to grant new licences in limited numbers, the massive population growth initially outstripped the supply of public houses. In 1830, however, the Beerhouse Act removed the limitation and allowed any householder who could pay an excise fee of two guineas to set up a business for the sale of beer. In common with many other places where the supply of drinking places had been restricted, Bradfordians took advantage of this business opportunity in impressive numbers. Within a decade, there were as many beerhouses, or beershops as they were also known, as there were houses licensed by the magistrates and by 1869 there were about 460 beershops compared to nearly 140 licensed houses. A number of the pubs illustrated in this book started out as beerhouses and many remained so, although at various times, the magistrates were willing to grant full licences to some and so enable them to sell wines and spirits. During these years, to take advantage of this licence, many fully-licensed houses turned their premises, either wholly or in part, into dram shops or gin palaces. These displayed the palatial fixtures and fittings in wood, tile and glass which have become the epitome of the Victorian pub.

The coming of railways prompted the demise of coach travel; trading stopped in the Piece Halls and older inns had to look to alternative sources of revenue – selling spirits in attractive surroundings was one option. Many beerhouses, in contrast, traded in rather more humble surroundings – often just two or three rooms with bare floors and simple furnishings.

In 1869, the law changed to require beerhouses to obtain a licence from the magistrates. That August, the bench took the opportunity to close sixty of Bradford's beerhouses, mostly due to police evidence of crime, prostitution and general disorderliness. In Southgate, then Bradford's most notorious street, four beerhouses were closed. One of these was Uncle Tom's Cabin, four connecting houses of which were said to be occupied by prostitutes. From 1869 onwards, licensing policy continued to be strict and very few new licences were granted; only substantial commercial premises like the Northgate or Rawson Hotels in John Street were exceptions to this. At the same time, redevelopment of the town saw the demolition of public houses, particularly of beerhouses, very few of which were replaced.

In 1904, legislation was passed which allowed for the closure of pubs that were no longer required, compensation being paid to the owner and licensee. Under this scheme, many beerhouses closed; the number of pubs had fallen to 351 by 1920, the split between beerhouses and full-licences being about even.

Just as Bradford was a Victorian creation, so too were the pubs themselves. The former hierarchy had given way to a more homogeneous institution – the pub – and customers were the working class; gentlemen who once patronised the Bowling

Green or the Sun now had their clubs and stagecoach travellers used railway hotels like the Victoria or the Midland. There was still an enormous variety of pubs. The big city centre gin palaces were at one end of the scale and little local beerhouses converted from private houses were at the other end. Internally too there was variety. There were the commercial, smoke and billiard rooms of the large multi-roomed establishments, then smaller pubs which consisted only of a parlour and tap room. One thing they all increasingly shared, however, was being tied to a particular brewery company, that is owned or leased by it and compelled to sell its products. Some of these breweries were Bradford based, such as Hammonds, Heys, Wallers or Whitaker & Co. but breweries from outside the town also acquired pubs there, like Stocks of Halifax. The name of the pub and its brewery owner came to be spoken of together – a Hammond's or a Hey's house.

The First World War was important in the history of drink and the pub in a number of ways. Britain became more sober as a nation, drink became more expensive and beer became weaker. Some features of pub life were introduced at this time and endured for much of the century. These were notably closing until late morning and again for a break in the afternoon. In post-war years, the licensing magistrates continued their strict policies and with the massive slum clearance programmes in inner Bradford, the number of beerhouses continued to decline. There were 180 in 1920 but by 1940 this number had dropped to 120. No new licences were granted, although in a handful of cases a beerhouse licence was upgraded to a closed full-licence. The White Hart in Thornton Road was one such example; it was transferred to the Albert Hotel in Manchester Road in 1929, and was renamed the Majestic. The justices resolutely refused to allow any pubs for the twenty-six new council estates, in which over 10,000 new homes were built. Only on appeal was one case successful – the transfer of a licence in White Abbey to the Lane Ends Hotel at Five Lane Ends in 1930.

Eventually after the Second World War, licensing policy did begin to be liberalised. Beerhouses were increasingly now granted a full licence. Coupled with the further massive slum clearance schemes carried out by the council this reduced their numbers still further, and by 1973 only four were left: the Artillery Arms in Bowling Back Lane, the Jacob's Well in Kent Street, the Parry Lane Tavern and the Woolpack in Whetley Hill, with the first on this little list the last to go. And, in contrast to the inter-war years, the new housing estates of the 1950s and 1960s were now provided with pubs by the surrender of the inner-city licences: the New Inn in Tyrrel Street, for example, for the Cap and Bells in Cooper Lane, Buttershaw. Finally, in more recent times, there has been the grant of some complete new licences.

Some pubs have undergone rebuilding. The New Beehive in Westgate is one such example. Built in 1901, it retains much of its original internal layout today. Examples from the inter-war years are the Old Crown in Ivegate and the Barrack Tavern at Bradford Moor, both built in 1928. From the 1960s, pubs include the Airedale in Otley Road and the Craven Heifer in Manchester Road.

More common were the alterations made to existing premises, notably by brewers Heys to create some interesting pubs. Internally, pub layouts continued to be multi-roomed, with better fixtures and fittings reflecting generally improving living standards. In the 1970s, pubs began to open out, creating the larger spaces we are familiar with today. Another change was in pub ownership; a smaller number of companies began to dominate pub ownership. This movement predated the First

World War but intensified in the 1950s. Already by 1940, Wallers had been taken over by the Leeds and Wakefield Brewery (Melbourne); Whitaker & Co. had ceased brewing, its brewery premises becoming the site of the New Victoria Cinema and its pubs being supplied by Tetleys of Leeds; and only Hammonds and Heys were still brewing at their Manchester Road and Lumb Lane sites. In the 1950s and 1960s, they too ceased brewing. Hammonds set off on the merger path that eventually led to Bass Charrington and Heys was merged with Websters of Halifax. Tetleys, with the takeovers of Melbourne and of Ramsdens of Halifax, increased its presence in the city. In more recent times, the brewing industry has been pulling out of pub ownership altogether.

Such massive changes inevitably generate nostalgia but nostalgia over pubs is not new to Bradford. In 1886, a local writer, James Burnley, presented a picture in the local paper, the *Bradford Observer*, of a group discussing how the council 'in taking away the slums and widening the streets [have] also destroyed some of the finest old Yorkshire pubs that ever existed'. The article goes on to dispute what year the so-and-so was pulled down and who the last landlord was and like matters. Burnley also knew of the darker side of pub life, which we should not forget. He visited a beershop in White Abbey, with a flagged and sanded floor, where '"drunk and disorderly" seems to be the motto of the establishment'. He records how two women started to fight near closing time and were ejected, two men later taking up their quarrel. As Burnley passes on, 'sounds of weeping women and cursing men, shrieking children and howling dogs, came to my ears...and I arrived at the conclusion that, let us improve our slums away as much as we may, slummy people will still continue to exist and men and women will congregate in wickedness and wretchedness'.

The pub has been and still is a complex institution, with dark as well as light in its makeup. Despite this, for the nineteenth and much of the twentieth century, the pub was the most important social centre for working people. It was mostly a getaway for men but the frequency with which women could be found in the pub in the past is greater than is often thought. Furthermore, the pub provided employment behind the bar for many women as well.

The images in this book and their accompanying captions not only try to show what pubs were like, but also convey something of the life they contained. My sources of information are many and varied. They include local newspapers, trade directories and the details of the censuses and licensing records, all of which are held at Bradford Central Library. Further licensing records are held at the West Yorkshire Archive Service office in Wakefield, together with the records of the former Bradford borough police, which include registers of licensed victuallers and beerhouse keepers, for which permission to view is needed. Local government building plans and the title deeds to some pubs are held at the Bradford office of the West Yorkshire Archive Service. Deeds for many demolished properties are held also by Bradford Council. When I did my research, deeds were also held by brewery companies, most of whom allowed me to look at them, but with the changes in pub ownership, these must now have been dispersed and are consequently likely to be more difficult to track down. They can, however, be enormously useful and in addition to details of ownership, they often contain maps, plans, inventories, auction particulars, copies of wills and brewery company information. Many individuals were also kind enough to share personal or family memories with me. Finally, for a detailed history using all of these sources and more, look at my book *The Public House in Bradford, 1770-1970*, published in 1995 by Keele University Press.

I have arranged the illustrations in this book topographically, beginning with the city centre then looking at inner Bradford, the home of so many working-class Bradfordians from the 1820s to the 1930s. I then look northwards before taking a clockwise course east, south and west of the central districts. Each chapter is prefaced by a short introduction to the area in question. One might think of it as a pub crawl in time.

Paul Jennings
*May 2004*

The four years since the publication of this book have continued to witness major changes in the pub world. By 2008, nationally twenty-seven pubs were closing every week according to the British Beer and Pub Association. They continued to be demolished, but many were also converted for other uses, such as private houses, flats, shops and restaurants. A combination of rising costs, falling sales, competition from home drinking, and other licensed premises, and in some cases the 2007 smoking ban, all contributed to the decline. Fundamentally, pubs had now become more of a financial asset for profitable use, rather than the traditional pub. For more detail of these and other recent changes, in the context of the long history of the pub, readers might like to turn to my book *The Local: A History of the English Pub*, published by The History Press in 2007. Bradford certainly has not been immune to these changes, as these pages will show. For this reprint I have made a small number of minor corrections and revisions.

Paul Jennings
*January 2009*

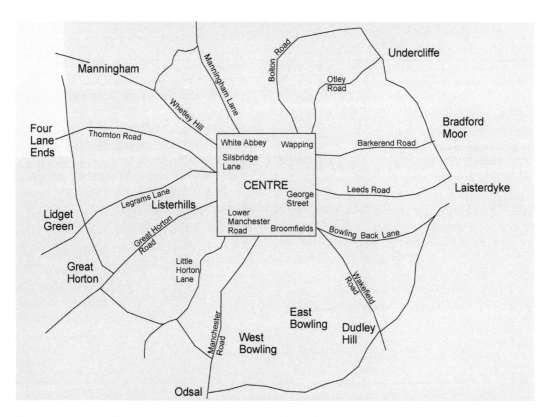

This sketch map of Bradford shows the main roads and localities.

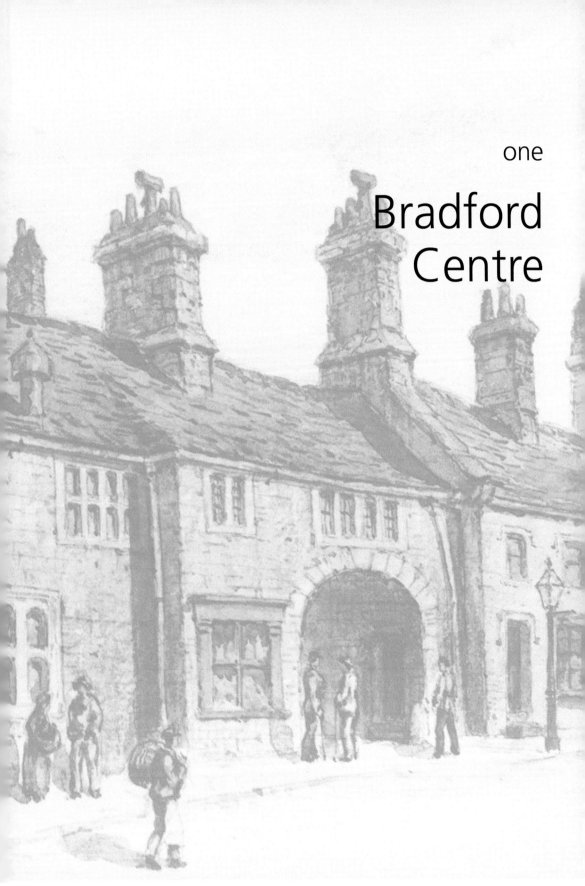

one

Bradford
Centre

The centre of Bradford has undergone three fundamental transformations in its history. One constant, however, has been the existence of the three ancient thoroughfares of Ivegate, Kirkgate and Westgate. To these three was added New, later Market Street, at the end of the eighteenth century. It was around this core area that the town developed in the first half of the nineteenth century, with densely packed housing and the new mills and warehouses intermingled. From 1850, this centre was transformed into the Victorian city with its great monuments: St George's Hall, the Wool Exchange, the Town Hall; imposing commercial buildings like those of Little Germany, the merchant quarter off Leeds Road and innumerable basic wool warehouses. In the course of this transformation, many of the old inns which served the town were demolished, like the Bowling Green for the Mechanics Institute opposite the Town Hall and the Sun for the new Prudential Insurance building at the bottom of Ivegate. To make way for Brown and Muff's new department store, the Roebuck, the Fleece and the Hope and Anchor disappeared, whilst on the other side of Market Street the Swan Inn made way for the arcade to which it gave its name. For the creation of Forster Square and the new Midland Railway station and hotel, the Bermondsey, the Brown Cow and the Church Steps Inns were levelled, whilst the progressive redevelopment of the west side of Westgate saw the removal of the Black Bull, Millergate, the Bull's Head, the Beehive, the Adelphi and the Bishop Blaize. Others survived into the twentieth century: the Druids, the Pack Horse and the Boy and Barrel on the east side of Westgate, or in Ivegate the Old Crown and the Unicorn and a small number of new, more substantial houses, like the Northgate and Rawson Hotels in John Street.

This essentially Victorian centre remained largely intact into the post-war period (Bradford having escaped relatively lightly during the war) as Pevsner was to observe in 1959 in his *Buildings of England*. There was only limited development in the inter-war years, including Britannia House or the New Victoria and Odeon cinemas. From then on, wholesale redevelopment effected the third transformation. This in its turn claimed more pubs, like the New Inn at the end of Thornton Road, the Empress in Tyrrel Street and the Granby in Union Street, though others were rebuilt, such as the Pack Horse in Westgate or the Queen in Bridge Street. In more recent times, there has been a steady drip of closures, for example, the Old Crown and the Unicorn, both in Ivegate. To offset these, liberalisation of licensing law from the 1960s permitted the growth of drinking in clubs and restaurants and latterly some new pubs have opened.

This photograph of the Bowling Green Hotel in Bridge Street is the oldest in the collection. The Hotel was rebuilt in 1750 and became one of Bradford's principal coaching inns. It was an important venue for political meetings; the Bradford Reform Society, for example, used the premises in February 1837 with Titus Salt in the chair; and in July 1852, it hosted the election dinner for friends of the Liberal candidates under the presidency of Samuel Lister. The bowling green itself was to the rear of the inn, near the stables and coach-house. It was demolished in 1871 and the Mechanics Institute was built on the site. The Institute in turn met the same fate a century later.

*Above:* The George Hotel in Market Street was originally a private house which opened as an inn in 1829 and was run for a long time by the Reaney family. It had a reputation as an artistic haunt, the local historian William Scruton calling it a popular venue for 'choicest specimens of local genius'. Charles Dickens stayed there in 1854 before a reading at the new St George's Hall. The hotel closed in 1919, the year this photograph was taken. At this time, it was described as 'one of the most comfortable commercial hotels in the city'. It was demolished for the extension of Bank Street.

*Right:* This shows the bar entrance at the rear of the George. It is an atmospheric photograph showing the kind of commercial premises which once covered much of central Bradford.

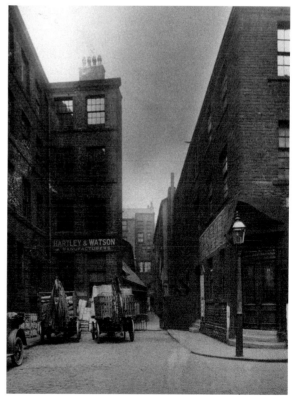

The White Swan Inn was on Market Street. It is shown here in one of N.S. Crichton's (1853–1913) watercolours, one of a number which he painted depicting old Bradford scenes. The White Swan was an important coaching inn. At the beginning of the nineteenth century, the landlord, John Bradford, was a coach proprietor and drove the Highflyer from York to Liverpool. The inn closed in 1876 but bequeathed its name to the arcade which was built on the site. The arcade was demolished a century later.

*Above:* The Iron Gates, as Albert Cowling's wine lodge was known, is to the left of this view of Market Street towards the Town Hall, photographed in around 1960. The name, dating from the First World War, succeeded earlier incarnations such as the Pineapple, the Salutation and the Griffin. Cowling, who died in 1952, also had the Sir Robert Peel in Westgate, the Prince of Wales in Bowling Old Lane and a wine lodge in Leeds.

*Right:* The Boar's Head, on the opposite side of Market Street, was an old inn dating back to the beginning of the nineteenth-century, which was rebuilt in 1872 by brewer Joseph Spink as a restaurant. Spink & Sons was later taken over by brewers Heys. Note Forster Square station to the right. Both sides of Market Street here were later demolished.

*Right:* The White Lion in Kirkgate was an old inn dating back to the eighteenth century, though the 1960 photograph here shows its later Victorian frontage with rather attractive lions' heads. It closed in 1963 and was demolished for new office premises.

*Below:* The first landlord of the Shoulder of Mutton on the opposite side of Kirkgate, John Wilson, was also a butcher – hence the pub's name. His daughter Elizabeth rebuilt the inn in 1825, a fact recorded above the doorway. To the left is the entrance to the former yard, which contained stables, wool warehouses and the inn's brewhouse. To the right of this photograph, taken in the mid-1980s, is the Midland Hotel, which provided rather more luxurious accommodation than the 'beds reserved for commercial gentlemen' at the Shoulder.

*Above:* The Talbot in Kirkgate was one of the leading inns of the town, photographed here not long before it was replaced by a new hotel in 1878. In Bradford's elections, it was the headquarters of the Tories and, more generally, it witnessed important events in the town's history. In 1830, the worsted spinners met to consider Richard Oastler's famous letter to the *Leeds Mercury* on child slavery in the town's mills. They called for a limit of eleven hours a day and eight on Saturday for children under fourteen. Note the wooden Talbot dog above the entrance. The new hotel had two fine stone specimens. That building remains, although it is no longer a hotel and the dogs have gone.

*Opposite above:* Another of Crichton's watercolours here shows the Beehive in Westgate, formerly the Horse and Groom, a change of name possibly occurring after landlord William Oldfield was sentenced to death for the murder of his wife there in 1820. In the event, he was reprieved in rather controversial circumstances. The Beehive was demolished in 1865. The building which replaced it at the corner of Godwin Street has a beehive carved on its façade as a reminder.

*Opposite below:* The first beerhouse in the collection is Southgate's Duchess of Kent, built by William Brayshaw in 1849 in the hope that it would be licensed. The licensing bench were not forthcoming until 1874. The street was later renamed Sackville Street. Brear & Brown of the Hipperholme Steam Brewery bought the Duchess of Kent in 1889 and it eventually passed to Tetleys, as may be seen when this photograph was taken in the mid-1980s. In 2008 it stood closed and boarded up.

Alf Leach (perhaps the one with moustache standing in the doorway with his staff) was the landlord of the Pack Horse in Westgate from 1903 to 1906. The Pack Horse was another old Bradford inn showing late Victorian embellishments. To the right is the Boy and Barrel, another old inn, and to the rear is the Manor House in Northgate. This beerhouse closed in 1917, although the building survives. The Boy and Barrel still trades, whilst the Pack Horse was demolished in 1966 and rebuilt on the same site.

*Above:* A little beyond the Pack Horse was the Druids Arms in Westgate, photographed here when the adjoining buildings had been removed to widen John Street, *c.* 1902. It was formerly noted as a popular spot with wrestlers such as Black Butcher Johnson who appeared at the Olympia in Thornton Road. A Hammond's house, it closed in 1966 and the building was demolished for new shops.

*Right:* The Northgate Hotel in John Street was purpose-built by brewer James Hammond and licensed in 1871. It was described as a second-class hotel with commercial, coffee and private sitting rooms. It was demolished in the major redevelopment of the area which also created the new market. Maybe the owner of the ladder had just popped in for a pint.

*Left:* The old Star Inn was rebuilt by Hammonds in 1897, as may be seen on the building, when this side of Westgate was widened. Its imposing frontage was photographed here in the mid-1980s.

*Below left:* A plan of the interior of the Star when it opened. Note the island bar arrangement serving all the rooms. This layout had become popular in larger pubs by this time. Note how the older term 'parlour' had given way to 'sitting room' and the existence of a dedicated bottle entrance, among three in total, for off-sales.

*Opposite above:* The rear of the Albion in Ivegate in 1892. John Barraclough & Co. traded there as brewers and wine and spirit merchants. The business failed in 1907 but continued under another name until 1941 when it was taken over by Yates Brothers and became one of their wine lodges.

*Opposite below:* William Richardson was the landlord of the Old Crown in Ivegate from 1884 to 1888. Local writer James Burnley described this music saloon as packed with listeners 'much in need of oxygen' enjoying 'two neatly attired young ladies' playing a duet. The old inn, which dated back to the eighteenth century, was rebuilt in 1928 and in later life was known for the young ladies there who wore no attire at all. It has now closed and is being put to other uses.

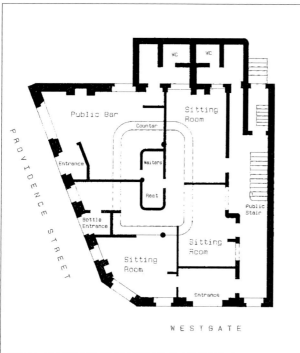

Jonas Dawson was born on Christmas Day in 1834. Shortly after his marriage to Dinah in 1862, the pair went into the pub trade, eventually taking the Unicorn in Ivegate in 1875. Jonas seems to have been a convivial character; he was a creditable singer and won prizes when he showed ponies at agricultural shows. In October 1878 his pony and trap was involved in an accident. By then he was already suffering from cancer of the liver which killed him the following year. He is buried in Undercliffe cemetery and his impressive granite monument bears a small engraving of a unicorn.

Jonas Dawson's widow, Dinah, continued to run the Unicorn until 1890. James Burnley described it as 'the resort of prosperous tradesmen, prosperous clerks, and prosperous betting men'. Tetleys bought it in 1900 in an early Bradford acquisition. This photograph, taken in the mid-1980s, shows its rather impressive frontage, particularly imposing as it is in such a confined space, the pub having been rebuilt in the mid-1820s. The Unicorn retained a rather old-fashioned city-centre pub atmosphere until its closure in the late 1980s when the original facade was destroyed.

The Queen in Bridge Street started life as a beerhouse named the Peel's Arms after its landlord but seems to have developed regal pretensions after being granted a full licence in 1851. The original Queen, whose building dated back to the eighteenth century, closed in 1964, three years after this photograph was taken. It was demolished and replaced by the new Queen.

Photographed here in 1961 when it was sold to the Bradford Corporation, this is the Granby Hotel in Union Street, which ran from Hall Ings to Nelson Street. The pub itself dated back to the 1830s and the entrance to the former yard with its stabling and coach-house is visible. The Granby and the surrounding area were razed for what became the Norfolk Gardens, a hotel and a car park.

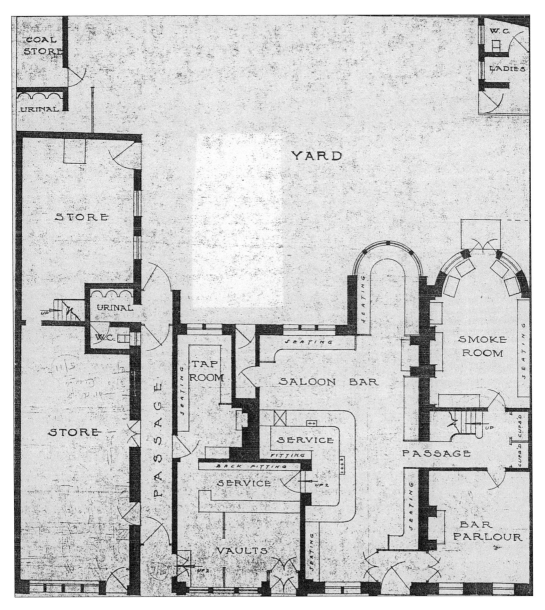

The interior plan of the Queen when it was purchased by Hammonds for £16,000 in 1914. Note the five separate rooms, each with its own designation and character. This was the universal practice in pubs until late in the twentieth century. Vaults in Bradford usually meant spirit vaults, that is, they specialised in selling spirits, although the term was also used to describe a basic tap room.

Local historian William Cudworth records that the New Inn was built in 1810, although an inn of that name is referred to in newspapers before then. In any case, the Bradford Assembly was held there in January 1811 and the inn was an important venue for meetings of all kinds, including magistrates' petty sessions. Photographed here in 1950, its former location at the end of Thornton Road may be gauged from the tower of the New Victoria cinema.

The interior plan of the New Inn when the Corporation bought it in 1920 with the intention of using the site for a new municipal theatre. This never happened but the next time the New Inn was not so lucky; it closed in 1964 and the licence was transferred to the Cap and Bells at Buttershaw.

*Opposite above:* When it opened in 1898 as a replacement for the old Commercial Hotel, the Empress (Queen Victoria was Empress of India) was Hammond's flagship house in Bradford. It was designed by the London pub architects Bird and Walters and, according to the local newspaper, its lavish internal fittings combined to create 'undoubtedly one of the most handsome and well-furnished buildings of its kind in Bradford'. This photograph was taken in around 1960.

*Above:* The Empress closed for trading in 1972 and was demolished the following year. Its demise saw the loss of a pub which brimmed with character; certainly, this is how I remember it from my observations as a youth from my Tyrrel Street bus stop. Its replacement is seen here in the mid-1980s from its Sunbridge Road entrance. Behind it is the Provincial building. Both it and the pub were later demolished.

Peter Bussey (1805–1869) was a beerseller and publican but also a radical. In the 1830s, he championed the relatively poor local beerhouse proprietors, contrasting them with the capitalists among the licensed victuallers. His politics occasioned a move to the United States of America, though he returned and became the landlord of the Fleece Inn at Horsforth. He is recorded as a USA citizen on his grave in Farsley church yard.

two

# Inner Bradford

The decade witnessing the fastest rate of growth in Bradford's population was the 1820s, which also saw the beginning of major housing developments around the central area. For thirty years, such houses were put up mostly back-to-back in courts, without any form of official regulation, many just one-up and one-down, unwatered except for a pump in the yard, the only toilet a communal privy. These housing developments were in the George Street area between Leeds and Wakefield Roads; Broomfields on the other side of Wakefield Road; the streets at the lower end of Manchester Road; the districts adjoining Silsbridge Lane, perhaps the poorest and most notorious of all; the streets on either side of White Abbey Road, and the Bolton Road and Wapping districts. A mix of people moved here; there were those who moved from villages surrounding Bradford or the rest of Yorkshire and others who travelled from Ireland. Many pubs were supplied for their use; it was the 'quickest way out' as the saying had it. By the 1850s there were seventeen pubs in the George Street district, fourteen of them being little beerhouses. In White Abbey in the 1880s, in the short stretch between Lumb Lane end and the Victoria in Wood Street, there were six pubs. It was no wonder that, as James Burnley noted, 'policemen walk in twos in White Abbey'. Neither the neighbourhoods nor any of those pubs remain today. The same is true of the other districts, some of which were demolished in the late nineteenth century. Sunbridge Road was created in the 1870s to form a new link to the west and this cut through many slum properties. Similarly, the building of Nelson Street as a new road to the south saw housing replaced by warehouses in the area to the east of Manchester Road. At the turn of the century, the Longlands area off Silsbridge Lane was cleared and Grattan Road was created off which the city's first council houses were built. A greater transformation came in the inter-war years when the remainder of these districts were swept away. In White Abbey, according to the inquiry held in 1923 into the improvement scheme, 2,300 people lived in 10.5 acres, and one in five of them were children under eight. It was described as 'one of the most unhealthy spots in the city', with forty per cent of houses still using old-fashioned privies. Many residents were nevertheless reluctant to move whether it was to the new housing proposed for the site, to Longlands or to the new Lower Grange estate. With the area went the pubs. Of the four affected: the Victoria, the Springfield, the Scott and White Abbey hotels, only the former was rebuilt as the Melbourne.

The Ring O' Bells derives its name from its proximity to the parish church. It was originally a private house in the Balme family (hence the street opposite) dating back to the late eighteenth century. In 1845, just thirteen days after the death of his first wife, the Ring O' Bells' landlord John Howard married a Miss Walker. She jilted her betrothed in order to commit to this marriage. The community showed its disapproval by blowing whistles and beating old tin cans outside the pub. This photograph is from the mid-1980s. The extension to the left was originally added to become a dram shop, specialising in the sale of spirits.

An early photograph of the Masons Arms in Stott Hill taken around the time it was closed for demolition in 1888. The beerhouse had been opened in 1845 by Robert Fearnley, who converted it from four old cottages to create a tiny two-roomed pub. It was common for publicans to have two occupations and Fearnley was no exception. He worked as a stonemason and so his wife Hannah no doubt did most of the work in the pub! The rear of the property overlooked the parish churchyard, the entrance to which is on the left. Note the urinal against the outside wall.

*Opposite:* Taken in the mid-1980s, this building was formerly the Sun. Situated at the corner where Cross Sun Street meets Captain Street, this Wapping district pub closed in 1907 under the provisions of the 1904 Licensing Act. Several other Wapping pubs were closed at this time, such as the Army and Navy, the Clarenton, the Old Armchair and the Duke of Edinboro' all in Bolton Road. They were declared as having inferior accommodation, being no longer needed and not good for police supervision.

Where Stott Hill meets Bolton Road was the tiny Fire Brigade, or Firecat as it was known. One of the longest pub-connected families was the Hinchliffe family; James Herbert succeeded his father James there in 1897 and stayed for over fifty years. The Firecat had been a beerhouse for a century when it closed in 1963, a few years after this photograph was taken.

Another tiny beerhouse was the Brown Cow in Wellington Street, converted from two cottages and originally known as the Horsfall's Arms from the nearby mill of that name. Tetleys of Leeds, in another early Bradford purchase, bought it in 1897. Cornelius Lane was there in the 1930s. It closed in 1943.

## BRADFORD.

### TO BE LET,

*(From Year to Year, or for a Term of Years.)*

ALL THAT WELL-ACCUSTOMED INN, or PUBLIC-HOUSE, situate in Wharf-street, and known by the sign of the Wharf Hotél, and within five minutes' walk of the town. The above house is well situated for carrying on an extensive business. The house consists of six Rooms on the ground floor—namely, Tap Room, capable of accommodating 50 persons, two good Kitchens, two neat Parlours, and a very convenient Bar. The Chambers consist of four excellent Bed Rooms, and a large Chamber, which accommodates a society of 135 members; this Room is so constructed that it can be made into two Lodging Rooms if required. There are also good Servants' Rooms in the Attic. The Outbuildings consist of a Butchers' Shop, and a complete Brewhouse, Malt Chambers, Gighouse, and a five-stand Stable, capable of accommodating 10 horses. There is a large Room over the Stable, Brewhouse and Gighouse, 20 yards long, well-finished and now used as a Lodge Room. There is excellent Cellering, and a never-failing supply of capital water on the Premises.

The above house has only been erected three years, and is well-finished, and has every requisite convenience.

The person taking the above Inn will be required to take the Stock and Furniture at a fair Valuation.

\*.\* For Rent and other Particulars apply personally or by letter, post paid, to Mr. SAMUEL KNOWLES, the owner, on the Premises.

The reason of Mr. Knowles retiring from business is on account of his health.

This 1837 advertisement for the sale of the Wharf Hotel is typical of many found in local newspapers. Note how the thriving lodge is used as an incentive to prospective purchasers.

By the mid-1980s the Wharf had become the Corn Dolly, as seen in this view of a now-empty Bolton Road; the houses, shops and pubs that once lined it have disappeared. To the left is the old Drayman Inn, which had been renamed the Goldsboro in 1926. The Drayman originally began when William Murgatroyd, who rebuilt the premises in about 1878, ran a small brewery there.

The Junction of Leeds Road and Vicar Lane was a classic corner pub which opened sometime in the early 1830s. According to theatre historian Peter Holdsworth, after the opening of the Bradford Civic Playhouse, for a time it became 'one of the best known theatrical pubs in the land'. It was still pretty theatrical in 1986, when this photograph was taken, just before it closed and was demolished for road development.

A plan of the Junction in 1890 when Waller & Son paid £9,200 for it. The plan shows the three original entrances still visible in the photograph. The original interior survived well into the twentieth century before it was remodelled and opened out.

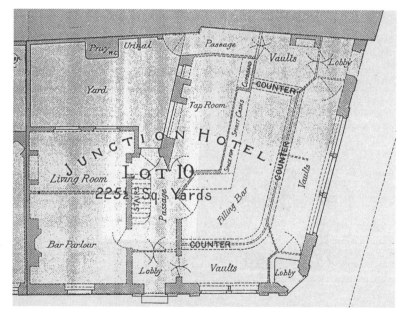

The Great Northern at the bottom of Wakefield Road in 1960, with the Adolphus Street goods depot behind. The Great Northern was a rebuild of an old beerhouse called the Farm Yard Inn. It was granted a full licence in 1898. Around the turn of the century, the Orrell family ran it and brewed there. When Arthur Orrell died in 1910, he was described as one of the best-known characters in Bowling, perhaps due to his enormous weight; he weighed some twenty-two stone. The Great Northern was demolished in 1987 for road development.

Another Wakefield Road pub was the Royal. At the intersection with Adolphus Street, this photograph, also taken in 1960, shows the pub two years before its closure. Licensed in 1852, a 1908 sale plan shows a substantial pub with commercial, smoke and tap rooms, vaults, a snug, a club or concert room and a billiard room.

On the other side of Wakefield Road is the Bedford Arms. This is another 1960 photograph, taken when the Arms was a Ramsden's of Halifax house. The pub is still standing although the Broomfields district that it served is long gone and much of the rest of the area is given over to roads. It was outside this pub on Boxing Day in 1876 that John Johnson shot and killed his best friend Amos Waite over Johnson's lover Amelia Sewell. Records state there had been an episode in the pub involving some ribaldry about the measurement of her thigh. Johnson expiated this tawdry tragedy on the gallows at Armley gaol.

*Above:* Charles Robinson opened this eponymous beerhouse in 1853 and was granted a full licence in 1868. Robinson's Hotel also served the Broomfields district in Moody Street. A Hammond's house, when it closed in 1952 it was reportedly the last building standing in the area.

*Right:* The Exchange Inn at the junction of Mill Lane and Fitzwilliam Street. A Hey's house, the brewers carried out characteristic alterations to it in the late 1920s sometime after this photograph was taken. Is that landlord Preston Stott peering from the side door?

*Above:* On the opposite side of Manchester Road to the Oddfellows pub stood the Alexandra Hotel, the Little Alex, as it was better known, another idiosyncratic Hey's alteration. It adjoined the Palace and Prince's theatres, which naturally provided custom from patrons and artists. One actor in particular is remembered as always ordering a bottle of Guinness for a 'quick one' between acts. When playing Dracula he would come into the pub with his black cape and green painted face, remove his fangs and down it in one gulp. The Little Alex was closed and the licence given up in 1971 for the Holme Wood Bound, a new estate pub.

*Opposite above:* The original Oddfellows pub in Manchester Road opened in the early 1830s. Its name was not uncommon due to the use made of pub premises by friendly societies. Hammonds bought the Oddfellows in 1898 when the ground floor was described as having a large dram shop or vault, at the entrance of which this group is standing.

*Opposite below:* Hammonds rebuilt the Oddfellows in 1939, complementing the Odeon cinema adjoining it. After a comparatively short life, the pub closed in 1965 and both it and the cinema were demolished.

The Jacob's Well at the junction of Manchester Road and Kent Street is indeed a survivor, one of very few properties of its kind left in inner Bradford. It was originally a block of four back-to-back houses, the two on the left being converted to a beerhouse in 1830, the year that the Act allowing their creation came into being. The 1841 census records Jacob Dawson as the landlord, so its name blends both personal and biblical allusions. It is photographed here in the mid-1980s in its modern setting.

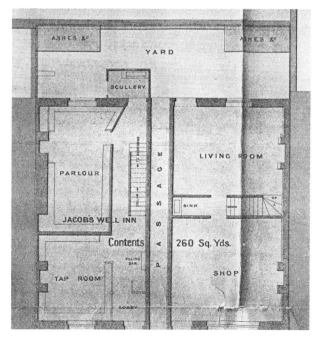

*Left:* This interior plan of the Jacob's Well in 1882 shows it as the small back-street beerhouse which it long remained; the precise arrangements were later altered to reverse the tap room and parlour and put the bar in the middle. It obtained a full licence in 1977 and expanded into the remainder of the property.

*Opposite:* The 1965 elevation and plan of the proposed Majestic in Manchester Road, a comparatively rare modernistic design. Note the continental touch of the roof terrace. This pub was to replace the older Majestic which stood at the bottom of Manchester Road but in the event was named the Yarn Spinner and is now gone.

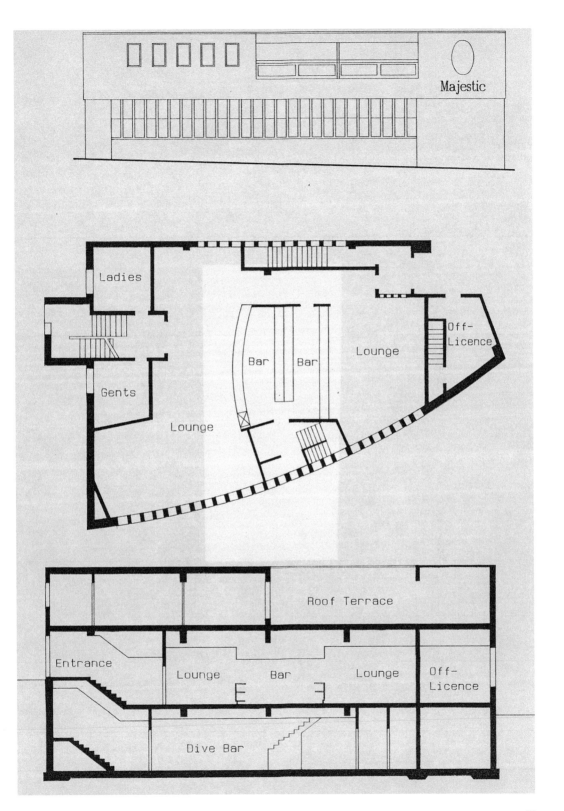

The Blue Lion at the corner of Manchester Road and Croft Street seen here in 1960. The older pub had been rebuilt in the late 1920s, set back from the road. My father recalled it being popular with rag and bone men who tethered their horses outside. It has now been demolished.

The King's Arms was also in Croft Street. It was rebuilt in 1890 when Nelson Street was created and nearby cottage property was replaced with warehouses. A policeman's surviving 1912 notebook describes visits to its concert room, where once fifteen men and seventeen women were seen singing comic songs to a piano accompaniment. The King's Arms was photographed not long after this time. It closed in 1949 and has been demolished.

The Greenwood brothers built the Caledonia Brewery on a street of the same name in 1890. Within six years, the business was absorbed into Boardman's United Breweries. The Greenwood brothers were subsequently voted off the board and Boardman's transferred production to the Denholme Gate Brewery. Boardman's never prospered and in 1921 sold their Yorkshire properties to Bentley's Yorkshire Breweries Ltd.

*Above:* Ready for their trip, the landlord and his friends pose outside the White Swan Inn. The landlord John Coyle is the man with the straw boater, moustache and buttonhole. He had taken the pub in 1892 and was noted as a boxing promoter. Prior to leaving on such trips, the men would throw pennies from the departing charabanc to the local children. The White Swan stood at the corner of Manchester Road and Duncan Street and closed in 1939.

*Opposite above:* The Ashley Hotel stood at the corner of two of the many terraced streets between Manchester Road and Little Horton Lane. It was a Stocks' house and George Lane had taken it in 1919. An earlier landlord Owen Lamb, who had left the police force as a result of a disability ('crippled' in the language of the day), was fined £25 for using the premises as a gaming house in 1898. He replied that he had done so because he couldn't make it pay. The Ashley Hotel finally closed in 1960.

*Opposite below:* As the photograph clearly illustrates, demolition was already under way around the Fitzgerald Arms when this photograph was taken. The Fitzgerald Arms was located in a street of that name which connected Manchester Road and Little Horton Lane. Crowther Street is to the right. The pub closed in 1960. Its licence and that of another Hey's pub, the Brunswick Hotel in Thornton Road were surrendered for a new house in Norman Lane at Eccleshill.

At the time of its construction and licensing in 1837, the Oddfellows Hall in Thornton Road was 'by far the largest public room in the town' It included a library, orchestra room and accommodation. By 1851, sixteen clubs held meetings there. It was photographed here in 1961. In 1963, it was designated as of special architectural and historic interest but in 1967 was sadly closed and demolished.

*Above:* It is not known what the button-holed occasion for this gathering was but many were certainly involved in this occurrence as can be seen from the group standing outside the splendid frontage of the Black Swan Tavern in Thornton Road in 1915 or '16. Landlord Arthur Gray is the man in the straw hat seated in the pony and trap, his son seated on the knee of a neighbouring publican. His wife, Sarah, holds the reins. Waller & Son bought the pub in 1870.

*Opposite below:* A pub which still stands is the Lord Clyde of Thornton Road, photographed here in around 1960. It took its name from a hero of the Indian Mutiny of 1857. It was owned by Whitaker & Co., whose brewery was at the end of Thornton Road. The Lord Clyde was hence ultimately a Tetley's pub.

Joshua Swithenbank of the Beehive Inn is the man in the apron at the corner of Tetley Street and
Grattan Road, the latter recently having been remodelled from the former notorious Silsbridge
Lane. The pub is also a grocer's shop; indeed Joshua so described himself in the census of 1891, and
this was not an uncommon employment combination at the time. In 1917, the magistrates deemed
dual businesses as objectionable and said that licences would only be renewed if the grocery was
given up. The Beehive had already closed in 1895, however, and had been demolished.

The Harp of Erin, pictured here in the mid-1980s at the junction of Chain and West End Streets, was one of a small number of pubs rebuilt in the decade before the First World War, in this case for brewers Waller & Son. At that time, the whole area known as Longlands, one of the poorest parts of Bradford, was being redeveloped with early municipal housing and this was to be the only new pub to serve its inhabitants. It was given its name by former landlord Patrick Henry, who was born in Ireland, but it no doubt pleased his many fellow countrymen and women who lived hereabouts.

The Melbourne replaced the Victoria Inn, built by Job Wood, hence the street's name, when the area was redeveloped. It opened in 1935, and according to the local newspaper, the site of the old pub provided a 'spacious forecourt for the parking of cars'. It was built for the Melbourne Brewery Co. of Leeds in a style used in several of their houses: 'brick with terra-cotta and rustic brick facings'. It is photographed here in 1995 by which time the name had been modified. It was later converted to other retail uses.

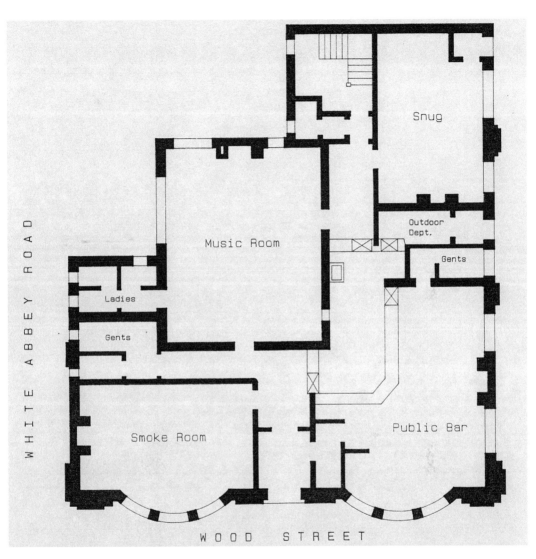

This internal plan of the Melbourne as it opened shows the traditional pub layout of separate rooms with familiar names. Also of interest are features like the chromium plating of this 'thoroughly modern and up-to-date suburban public house'. Clearly the brewery had high hopes for this area now that what had been condemned as a slum district a decade earlier had been developed with new council housing.

Alfred Perkins took on the Flying Dutchman in 1916. This pub, a beerhouse at the junction of Lumb Lane and King Street, was originally named after the celebrated racehorse. In 1911, a previous landlord had been reported to the police for allowing prostitutes to carry out their business there; at the time, local newspapers reported cases of brothels in this part of town and this serves as an early indication of the Lane's later notoriety. Heys altered the pub in the mid-1930s.

The Theatre Tavern in Manningham Lane was opened as a beerhouse in 1865; run by Mary Walker, it became known as Walker's Entire, but it later took its name from the Theatre Royal opposite. It was altered by Heys brewers and is photographed in the mid–1980s. It closed and was demolished after a campaign to save it from road development failed; at the time, it was claimed that the road would cut traffic levels on Manningham Lane by up to fifty per cent.

*Above:* This photograph of the Royal Standard in Manningham Lane is confirmation of a pub that the 1985 auction particulars described as 'in need of refurbishment'. The auctioneers also assured people that it was a 'reminder of the magnificence of Victorian architecture'. The building was originally a Turkish and slipper bath for John Thompson. In 1872, he gained a full licence for refreshment rooms for it. A waitress who worked in its smoke room providing matches for gentlemen to 'light up' was charged in 1873 with attempting to set the place on fire but the case was dismissed. The Royal Standard eventually caught fire and was demolished in 1991.

*Left:* The entrance to the Royal Standard shows its mosaic floor. To the left of the entrance was a large room that, in the late 1970s, was a punk rock venue.

*Above:* The splendid vaults of the Royal Standard etched on the glass of the door. An interior like this surely epitomises what a pub should look like.

*Right:* The Royal Standard's toilets were equally splendid as the rest of the venue.

The property in the centre of this photograph was part of the Victoria Street development carried out by the Bradford Second Economical Building Society. John Beanland set up in business as a grocer and beer retailer in two houses which he bought in 1861, one of which faced Manningham Lane. In 1918, Robinson Turner took over the Bradford Arms from Joseph Dunbavin, a star player for Bradford Northern Rugby Club. The Bradford Arms was one of several pubs acquired by Hammonds in their purchase of brewers J.R. Holmes & Sons the following year. Joseph Richard, a former partner of William Whitaker & Co. established the new brewery in 1890 by the canal at Dowley Gap in Bingley.

The Trafalgar Brewery of Waller & Son Ltd in Trafalgar Street off Manningham Lane, as pictured in the *Brewers Journal* on 15 January 1908. The illustration shows the new maltkiln and extensions to the pneumatic maltings. When the brewery was originally built in 1853, it was done so purposefully close to the railway. Brewing was later transferred to the brewery of Brear & Brown of Hipperholme and the company was taken over by the Leeds and Wakefield brewery in 1935. The premises survived until demolition in 1953, having been bought for the building of a through railway connection for Bradford which never came.

# WALLER & SON, LIMITED,

## · · BREWERS, · ·

## Wine & Spirit Merchants,

### HAVANA CIGAR MERCHANTS,

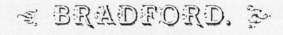

## WALLER'S L.B, ALE

AND

# NOURISHING STOUT,

## IN SCREW-STOPPERED BOTTLES,

**2/6**    Imperial Pints    **2/6**

Per dozen.                      Per dozen.

THE BEST IN THE MARKET.

## SMALL CASK OF BEER for family use, in splendid condition

### 1/-, 1/2, and 1/4 per gallon.

Quality unsurpassed.

## WALLER'S CREAM OF SCOTCH, a very fine old Liqueur

A late 1890s' advertisement for Waller & Son's products. Note the small casks of beer for family use.

three

North

The only flat route out of Bradford is along the valley of the Bradford Beck, which flows down to the River Aire at Shipley. The others are up hills. The steep pull past the parish church, now the cathedral, branches off at North Wing by the seventeenth-century Paper Hall, which miraculously is still there. This led through Wapping on one side and lower Otley Road on the other. There were once plenty of pubs here, for example, the Fox and Hounds or the Stone Lion in North Wing, which both closed at the beginning of the 1960s. Along Wapping Road, there were once three: the Union Cross, the Richmond House and the Gardeners Arms. From 1874 to his death in 1882, the landlord of the Gardeners Arms was Matthew Hughes, one of the first winners of the Victoria Cross for his bravery in the Crimean War in 1855. This fact, however, cut no ice with the licensing magistrates when he asked for a full licence for his beerhouse. Hughes, like many other Bradford landlords and landladies, has a last resting place in Undercliffe cemetery towards which Otley Road climbs. The monument there to the land agent Joseph Smith is the perfect viewpoint across Bradford and to the Aire Valley. Directly across from the cemetery is Manningham Lane, which runs from Lister Park to the town centre. This route is a contrast to the lower reaches of Otley or Bolton roads with middle-class housing developments such as Blenheim Road, Apsley Crescent and Mornington or Walmer Villas facing or adjoining it. In the mid-1950s, the city's official handbook still noted the 'procession of gleaming aristocratic cars' coming down Manningham Lane into the city. But this isn't really pub territory, unlike the other main roads into the city. Manningham itself was more working class. The original village was along Church Street and Heaton Road and had more pubs like the New Inn, the Mowbray, the Bavaria, Springcliffe or Junction. Another pub-filled area was the western side of Lumb Lane, the advance of terraced streets having overwhelmed a middle-class development like Southfield Square. All but one of the Lane's pubs were found there: the Flying Dutchman, the Friendly, White Bear and White Swan, the Perseverance and the Queen's hotels (the exception being the Barracks). In addition, close to the junction with Marlborough Road in Wilson Square was Hey's brewery. This closed in the 1960s and has now been demolished.

The Cock and Bottle at the junction of Barkerend Road and Otley Road pictured here in 1960. The inn dated back to the eighteenth century and is a late example of a home brew pub into the twentieth century until it was acquired by Melbourne in the late 1920s. Note the company's trademark courtier over the entrance.

The pub was advertised for sale in 1901 as 'recently elaborately fitted up on the most modern principles', including this splendid entrance photographed here in the mid-1980s. It still retained at this time many 1901 features, and Tetleys designated it as a Heritage Inn. It was also used as a film set and apparently did a good trade, but in recent years its future has sometimes been uncertain.

*Above:* The Airedale, located where Otley Road meets North Wing, was licensed in 1848. In March 1889 it hosted the first annual dinner of the Airedale Musical Union. It was also here that in 1891 men of the district formed what became the East Ward Labour Club. The Cattericks took it in 1910 when this photograph was taken. When they left it in 1921, they were presented with a silver rose bowl on an ebony stand 'as a token of esteem and respect by their numerous friends'. The old pub was demolished in 1964 and replaced by a new one by Tetleys who owned it at the time; the whole area was simultaneously being redeveloped with new council housing.

*Opposite above:* Time was certainly about to be called at the Olive Branch in Otley Road when it was photographed here in 1960, the year before its closure. It then had a tap room, 'long stand-up', snug and singing room. It was, at this time, a Hammond's beerhouse, acquired by them in 1890.

*Opposite below:* Higher up Otley Road at its junction with Gaunt Street was the George, a basic cottage property with an embellishment to the main road. This was another simple beerhouse with a bar, tap room and singing room. It originally belonged to Whitaker & Co. and thus to Tetleys.

Charles Blakey took over the New Inn in Otley Road at Southampton Street in 1913. It became a Hammond's house in the Holmes purchase of 1919. It closed rather suddenly when it was found to be structurally unsound in 1974 and was subsequently demolished.

On the other side of Otley Road was the New Inn. It had originally been called the Knackers Inn as the landlord at the time was also in business as a horse slaughterer. Perhaps advisedly, it was renamed. It is seen here in the late 1960s with a later frontage added to the cottages from which it has originally been converted. It has now been demolished.

Daniel Riddiough originally opened the Peel Park in Otley Road in 1852 as the Undercliffe Hotel; its later name was taken from the adjoining public park, Bradford's first. This photograph was taken in 1960.

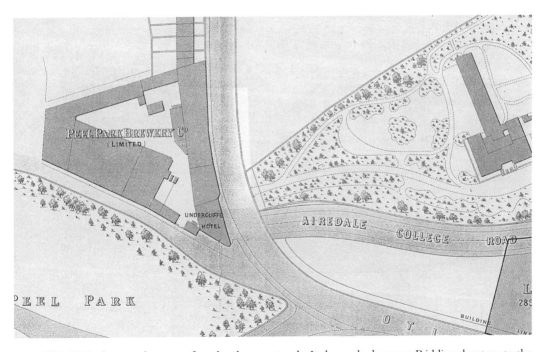

This 1879 plan was drawn up for a local property sale. It shows the brewery Riddiough set up to the rear of the pub; this brewery became a public company in 1872. It collapsed in 1882 in an 'utterly insolvent' state, although Riddiough later re-acquired it and it traded until it was sold to Hammonds in 1891.

*Above:* On the other side of Peel Park, Riddiough also owned the Bolton Hotel, which was built in 1858 and licensed the following year. The park was meant to be alcohol-free and contains several temperance monuments, but Riddiough clearly had an eye for business, placing large pubs at each entrance. The Bolton still retains its yard and stables.

A little further up Otley Road at Undercliffe is the Green Man, which dates back to the mid-1790s. Bought by Whitaker & Co. in 1820, it was one of the first public houses in the town to be bought by a brewery. In 1863, the company bought the cottages to the left and the pub was extended into them. This photograph of the Green Man was taken in the mid-1980s.

*Above:* Another old Undercliffe pub is the Hare and Hounds, also photographed in the mid-1980s. The Hare and Hounds was built in 1788 by Isaac Thornton who was nicknamed Huntsman according to his hobby; it is probably because of this that the pub was given this name. Thornton lived to eighty-two and his heirs eventually sold the pub to the Peel Park Brewery Co.

*Opposite below:* Hammonds also acquired the Beldon Hotel in Otley Road with its 1891 Peel Park Brewery purchase. The Beldon, a beerhouse until as late as 1961, remained virtually indistinguishable from a private house. It was granted a full licence the next year but closed in 1971.

*Above:* Taking its name from nearby quarries, the Delvers Arms in Bolton Road was close to its junction with Wapping Road. Arthur Boldy was the landlord from 1921 to 1925. The group in this photograph were ready for a charabanc trip. These trips dated back to before the First World War but grew enormously in popularity in the 1920s. Note the watch chains. Among the men are Tubby Caulfield, seen second from the left, Swallow Wood with the dented hat and Spratty Boldy with his dog. The pub closed in 1939.

*Opposite above:* On the other side of the valley is the Mowbray Arms in Lily Street on what looks like a sunny day in Manningham. Isaac Newton had taken the pub in 1902, a purpose-built house first licensed in 1852. It is now closed.

*Opposite below:* The Volunteer Hotel in Green Lane was gloomily pictured in the 1920s. The landlord John Slater drowned himself in the canal in March 1878, having left home three weeks before in low spirits and threatening so to do. The Volunteer Hotel was part of the Holmes & Sons purchase by Hammonds in 1919. It ceased trading in 1957 and was demolished in the general clearance of the Green Lane/Picton Street area.

The Spotted House on Manningham Lane, photographed in the 1890s, was once also called the Lister's Arms, from the family who owned the inn and the estate which eventually became Lister Park. J. B. Priestley recalled it as the pub he 'best remembered', and as 'a haunt of rare souls' with grand old woodwork and shining settles and tables, although he later grieved over the 'bogus plastic luxury that too many pubs provided for younger customers'. Owned for many years by the Tankard family, Hammonds paid £20,000 for the Spotted House in 1937. It had a bowling green, tennis courts and a pool whose vent may be seen to the right, and it was the headquarters of both the Airedale cycling and Manningham bowling clubs.

Samuel Clark built and opened the Belle Vue Hotel in 1874, although he didn't enjoy it for long as it was declared bankrupt four years later. It is seen here in a drawing showing the carriage folk in Manningham Lane; the drawing depicts when it was up for sale in 1890.

## LOT 3.

All that well-established HOTEL, known as the

# BELLE VUE HOTEL,

situate in Manningham Lane, Bradford, with the Club Rooms, Stables, Coach Houses, Yards, and other premises adjoining and belonging thereto. The site of the whole containing 1886 square yards or thereabouts.

The Hotel is an imposing edifice, very substantially built and commands a very important position. It is a thoroughly comfortable Commercial and Family Hotel, is very well frequented and doing a large and profitable business. It is also the Head-quarters of the Manningham Football and Cycling Clubs.

The Hotel contains on the Ground Floor a commodious Entrance and Hall, Refreshment Bar, Smoke Rooms, and Private Bar, large Bar Parlour and lofty well-lighted Billiard Room (two tables), also Filling Bar, Snug and Private Sitting Room, well-arranged Kitchens, Sculleries, and Store Rooms, large Tap Rooms and Vaults. It also contains large Commercial and Coffee Rooms on the First Floor, 21 Bed Rooms, Sitting Rooms, Bath, Lavatory, and W C., Store Rooms, &c.

The property is situated in the most frequented part of the town and Tram Cars pass every few minutes.

The 1890 sale particulars speak for themselves.

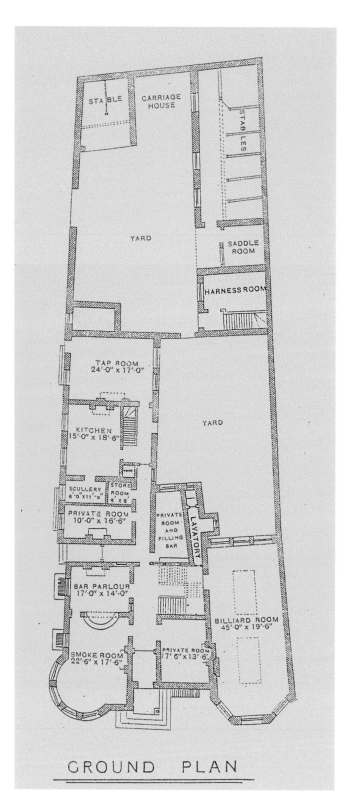

STABLE

CARRIAGE HOUSE

STABLES

YARD

SADDLE ROOM

HARNESS ROOM

TAP ROOM
24'-0" x 17'-0"

YARD

KITCHEN
15'-0" x 18'-6"

SCULLERY
6'-0" x 11'-0"

STORE ROOM
6' x 8'

PRIVATE ROOM
10'-0" x 16'-6"

PRIVATE ROOM AND FILLING BAR

LAVATORY

BAR PARLOUR
17'-0" x 14'-0"

BILLIARD ROOM
45'-0" x 19'-6"

SMOKE ROOM
22'-6" x 17'-6"

PRIVATE ROOM
17'-6" x 13'-6"

GROUND PLAN

The ground plan of the hotel as shown at the time of its sale. The sale was occasioned when the hotel's next owner also became bankrupt. In this sale, Hammonds bought it for £7,400. It latterly seemed to enjoy a good trade from football supporters visiting nearby Valley Parade and devotees of striptease, a market to which it catered. It has now closed and is put to other uses.

four

East

Where Otley Road branches off to the north, Barkerend Road, the old route towards Leeds, continues towards Bradford Moor. There were a few pubs in Barkerend Road's lower section, such as the Army and Navy which was demolished for the new ring road, or the Ivy, owned by Garnetts whose mills dominated the townscape, which has also been demolished. The Red House and the Barkerend survived them. Beyond the mills, much of the housing was built post-1869 when the grant of licences became restricted or, through restrictive covenants, the developers deliberately prevented property being used as pubs. Thus on both the eastern side of Barkerend Road around Harewood Street and on the western side which included the streets making up Poet's Corner – Tennyson, Shakespeare, Wordsworth and others – there were no pubs until Bradford Moor where the Cardigan Arms, the Barrack Tavern and the Coach and Horses could be found, the Coach and Horses dating back to the late eighteenth century.

A rather different picture is presented by other roads to the east such as the new Leeds Road which opened in the mid-1820s, Bowling Back Lane,and the industrial and working-class housing areas which were between them. Oddly the former road had no pubs on its western side between the Flying Dutchman at the bottom of Garnett Street and the Waggon and Horses at Thornbury. In contrast, the eastern side of the road had twenty pubs during the 1880s and included the Golden Lion, the New Exchange, the Adelphi, Waterloo, the Albion, the Oak, Cemetery, Lemon Tree, Victoria, St Leger, Wheatsheaf, White Bear, Napier and the Highflyer. At the same time, Bowling Back Lane had fifteen pubs along its route to Swaine Green, with the Forgeman's Arms or the Furnace deriving their names from the huge Bowling Iron Works. Other examples are the Eagle, or the Farmyard, where boxing was held, and the Upper Croft, the Bradford Arms and the Artillery. Mount Street, located in between Bowling Back Lane and Leeds Road, ran through another of Bradford's poor districts. Clarence Muff, a one time bookies' runner, recalled two local publicans as 'very good punters' in his memoirs. One of them, the landlord of the Gladstone Arms, allowed dice gambling after hours. According to Muff, the crafty customers were one step ahead of the gullible licensee who was eventually driven to do a moonlight flit as he owed money to the brewery. Bradford once had five pubs named after the great Victorian politician who once claimed to have lost an election because of a torrent of gin and beer provided by his drink trade opponents to thirsty voters. This particular Gladstone closed its doors in 1938.

Receiving its full licence in 1848, the Barrack Tavern on Killinghall Road at Bradford Moor took its name from the barracks built on the opposite side of the road. That old pub was rebuilt in 1927-28 in the rather bogus Tudor style adopted in those years by some brewers, in this case Bentley's Yorkshire Breweries. The style supposedly evoked Merrie England, and 'Ye' was formerly prefixed to the name. This photograph was taken in 1995. Ye Barrack Tavern has now closed and the building was converted to a restaurant.

The Red House in Barkerend Road at Garnett Street is a mid-nineteenth century beerhouse, built substantially with stables and a coach-house in the hope of getting a full licence. The entrance to the yard can be seen on the right of this mid-1980s picture. During the First World War, the landlady fell foul of the restrictive licensing climate of those years, first in August 1915 for not closing for sale to HM forces at 3.30 pm, and again in December for having children on the premises. They were actually mummers working their way around the pubs, but the bench still fined her ten shillings for each child.

The Barkerend, a little further down the road, opened as a beerhouse in 1864. It was bought by William Whitaker & Co. in 1897, and this same company remodelled the premises in around 1912 to their appearance here in the mid-1980s. By 2008 it was closed and boarded up.

This photograph of the New Inn, a typical beerhouse at the corner of Garnett Street and Joseph Street, was taken in 1960. It retained its old multi-roomed interior until quite late in its life. It has now closed, although the building remains.

On the opposite side of Garnett Street was The Garnett, a grocer's shop and beerhouse which began in around 1850. The pub has closed since this photograph was taken in the mid-1980s and the premises has been demolished.

Completing this neighbouring trio of pubs was the Flying Dutchman in Leeds Road. It was rebuilt by Hammonds in 1900 after they obtained a full licence for the beerhouse the previous year. The pub was a fine example of bold late-Victorian pub architecture. The former entrance to its jug and bottle department may be seen to the left. In this mid-1980s photograph, it is seen as a 'fun pub'. It was later demolished.

The building to the right was formerly the Eastbrook Hotel in East Parade, a Hammond's house. It closed in 1955 when it apparently sold only a little over a barrel of beer a week. It was eventually demolished in 1987 for the new ring road. The building to the left remains. It was originally Eastbrook House, a mansion standing in its own landscaped grounds, but Bradford's development engulfed it.

The New Market Hotel at the corner of Wenlock Street and Filey Street took its name from St James's Market, which was new when the pub was licensed in 1873. The New Market Hotel had a basement bar which opened in the early morning for market traders, but it became a magnet for early drinkers generally and allegedly the morning licence was withdrawn after a man died in a fight outside. The pub closed in 1964.

*Above:* A rather gloomy picture of the Artillery Arms in Bowling Back Lane in the late 1960s, with Parry Lane off to the right. This beerhouse had opened a century earlier and was in the heart of industrial Bradford with the Bowling Iron Works behind it and the Bradford Gas Works opposite. The pub took its name from a detachment of artillery volunteers formed at the Bowling Iron Works. When the landlady Doris Jackson retired in 1981, fifty-three years after she and her late husband Fred took it over, it was the last beerhouse in Bradford. The photograph shows it as a Richard Whitaker of Halifax house, later Whitbread, but in 1982 Trough Brewery of Idle bought it and to encourage more women to visit it, it finally got its spirit licence. The Trough Brewery sold it in 1987 and the pub is now closed.

*Opposite above:* The Cemetery Hotel, on the opposite side of Leeds Road to the cemetery itself, was licensed to Luke Brook in 1855. It was a Stocks' house when it was photographed here in the early 1920s. It is now closed and the building has been put to other uses.

*Opposite below:* A little higher up Leeds Road at Walnut Street, the Victoria Hotel was built substantially by John Barron with a view to a spirit licence, which it was granted in 1875. Part of the Holmes estate purchased by Hammonds in 1919, it has now closed, along with several other Leeds Road pubs.

This beerhouse was opened in 1844 and was originally a row of houses. It was appropriately known originally as the Cross Roads Inn (of Leeds and Killinghall Roads at Laisterdyke), before it changed its name to the Wheatsheaf. Photographed here early in the 1960s, note the delights of Australia beckoning in the distance. The licence was surrendered in 1969 to a new pub, the Moonrakers on Halifax Road, and the premises was demolished.

The Napier Inn, further along Leeds Road towards Thornbury, was formed from cottages in 1868. It was photographed when it was under the tenancy of Albert Clegg who had been its landlord since 1913. In the mid-1890s, this J.R. Holmes & Sons' house was the subject of a court case dealing with the power of the licensing magistrates with regard to alterations to licensed premises, something which was much disputed at the time. The nub of the issue was the right to sell drink in a new room which had been created since the original premises were licensed, seen here to the right. In this instance, the point was decided in the owner's favour but the power of magistrates over alterations was subsequently incorporated into the 1902 Licensing Act.

The Moulders Arms in Sticker Lane derived its name from its proximity to the Bowling Iron Works. John Hornby held its licence as far back as 1827. Seen here during its time as a Stocks' house, it was closed in 1982, by then shorn of buildings to right and left. It was demolished in spite of some controversy at the time over whether this should be done.

The Parry Lane Tavern, at its junction with Sticker Lane, was a beerhouse formed from several cottages in about 1859. As an example of the hysteria of the time, during the First World War, the licensee James Watson was branded akin to a traitor by a magistrate after he had allowed a member of the armed forces to drink outside time.

five

# South

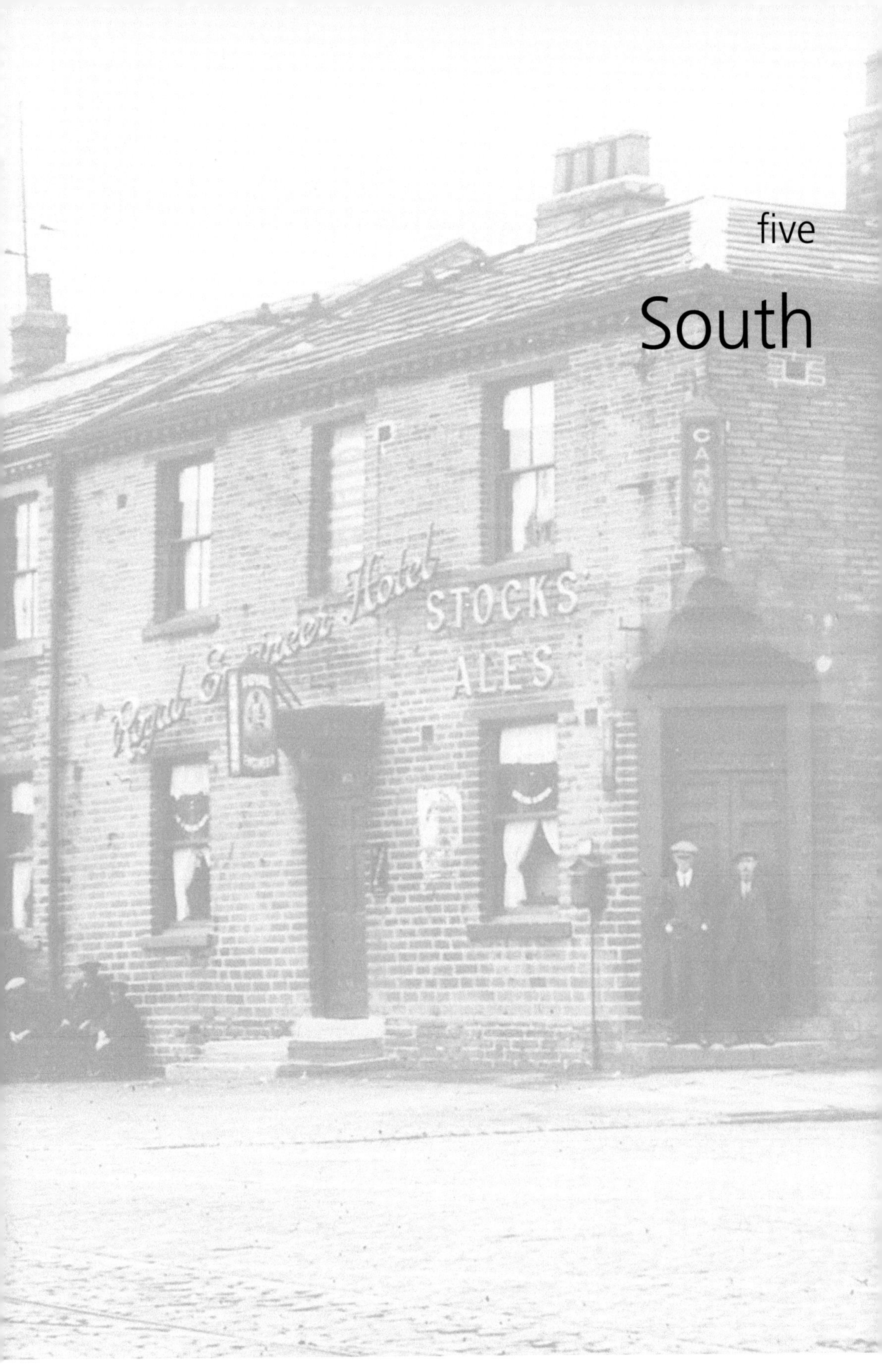

Like Leeds Road, Wakefield Road was once plentifully supplied with pubs, with more than twenty along its route from the Great Northern and the Bedford at its foot up to Dudley Hill. Some had rather quaint names like the Tichborne Arms, which immediately adjoined the Royal Hotel, and the Little Wonder, the Busy Bee and the Greenhouse. Manchester Road is best remembered however, as at the beginning of the last century, it had some thirty-five pubs between the city centre and Odsal, a route of not more than an hour's walk — so long as you didn't stop en route at any of the pubs! On such a walk, you would begin at the city centre end with the Albert later known as the Majestic, and the Oddfellows, and would go all the way up to Odsal with the Truncliffe Gate and the Fox and Hounds. Both Wakefield and Manchester Road and their adjoining districts were utterly, not to say ruthlessly, transformed by redevelopment in the 1960s and 1970s and very few of these pubs now remain. Dudley Hill and Odsal disappeared into vast roundabouts and underpasses and at many other points, it is difficult indeed to visualise what once was there. A small number of pubs were rebuilt: in Manchester Road, for example, the Majestic moved up the hill to become the Yarn Spinner, although this has now also gone and the Craven Heifer at the end of Smiddles Lane, which was set further back from the new road.

Manchester Road was once a new development. The original route followed Bowling Old Lane, making a more meandering way through the township of Bowling. The new stretch, built in the mid-1820s, provided a straighter road to the junction with Smiddles Lane. The other main route to the south, Little Horton Lane, has survived. Much of the middle-class housing built from the 1840s along the lower section still remains, as does the hamlet of Little Horton Green, a number of seventeenth and eighteenth century houses nestling in the impressive shadow of All Saints Church. Three very old inns punctuated Little Horton Lane's route up to Chapel Green and past Southfield Lane: the Red Lion which is still there, the Fox and Pheasant which exists albeit in an altered state, and the Black Horse which was rebuilt by Hammonds in 1876 as an impressive corner pub but which is now closed and has been put to other uses.

This photograph shows the Wheat Sheaf at the corner of Wakefield Road and Hall Lane in 1926. The Wheat Sheaf was an old inn dating back to the eighteenth century when it was part of the Bolling Hall estate and the venue for the meetings of the officers of Bowling township.

The Wheat Sheaf has been transformed in a characteristic style by the brewers Heys. The Victory Ale, named for its success in competitions, was certainly strong, with an original gravity of 1075°. The Wheat Sheaf has now been demolished.

The woman in the doorway is very likely Hannah Smith, the licensee of the Bowling Park Hotel in Wakefield Road from 1899 to 1906. Originally a beerhouse known as the Graziers Inn, it obtained a full licence in 1881 and changed its name to that of the new public park, the road to which may be seen at the left. The Bowling Park Hotel has now been demolished.

The Napoleon Hotel is still on Wakefield Road. It was originally a private residence called Upper House and was converted to a pub by Robert Ellenthorpe. It was granted a full licence in 1867 and was probably named after 'little' Napoleon III than the 'great' Emperor. The local police station was next door and apparently an inspector there would warn the landlord to take care over after-hours drinks when he was on leave. When the Bowling Tide fair was on, the custom never keeled day or night. Photographed here in 1960, the Napoleon Hotel had been a Hammond's house since 1889.

*Above:* Emma Hall was the licensee of the Church Hill Inn from 1916 to 1920 when it was a Stocks' house. At this time, the little beerhouse consisted of a tap room, best room and small singing room, and is remembered as doing a steady trade with many railwaymen or tram-men from the nearby shed. It was also the nightly refreshment call for the trio of musicians who accompanied the films at the Coventry cinema on the opposite side of the road.

*Opposite above:* The Greenhouse Inn in Wakefield Road opened as a beerhouse in 1867 and closed exactly 100 years later. It was a Hammond's house at the time this photograph was taken in 1960.

*Opposite below:* This photograph of Forster's Hotel at Wakefield Road and Busfield Street was taken in 1960. It began as a beerhouse and was granted a full licence in 1872. It once belonged to Waller & Son and so in 1960, was a Melbourne house. It has now been demolished.

The Royal Engineer at Dudley Hill had been a public house from the close of the 1820s and the brewer Michael Stocks paid £3,220 for it in 1869. By the time this photograph was taken in the 1920s, the former stables had given way to a garage. It was sold to the Bradford Corporation in 1967 for £23,544 and was demolished in preparation for a giant roundabout.

The Cross Keys Hotel in Rooley Lane was pictured here after 1918 when Ernest Cluderay was the licensee. The pub displays its new Hammond's signage, as the Cross Keys Hotel was acquired in the Holmes' purchase the following year.

The White Hart Hotel was also in Rooley Lane. It had been an inn from around 1800, when John Firth created it from a row of cottages. This photograph was taken during the time when Alice Wilson was licensee; she took it over in 1914.

This photograph of the Queens Arms at Caledonia Street and Manchester Road was taken in 1958. The Queens Arms was first licensed in 1838 and survived a gas explosion in 1855 when the roof was partly blown off. Unfortunately, it did not survive modern redevelopment and it closed in 1963.

The Oxford Hotel in Mill Lane was another Holmes' house acquired by Hammonds, and seen here with new sign. The Oxford Hotel closed in 1962, although the building remained rather forlornly for many years.

This image of the Fountain was taken in 1958. The pub stood at the corner of Manchester Road and Franklin Street (opposite Mill Lane if you want to get your modern bearings) with Hammond's brewery behind it. Both the pub and the brewery were bought by the Corporation in 1968 and were subsequently demolished.

The Albany Hotel at Manchester Road and Spring Mill Street was an early Webster's acquisition in the city. It is seen here having its front step scrubbed. The Albany was later demolished.

Hammonds United Breweries was created in 1946 to reflect the company's expansion beyond its Bradford base, and the resulting initials led to the wheel logo (also seen on the sign of the Fountain). This is an advertisement from the Bradford Official Handbook of the 1950s. Export Unity was a strong pale ale, whilst Guards Ale was an even stronger dark brew sold in one-third of a pint bottles known as 'nips'.

*Opposite:* Edward Dobson was an auctioneer, valuer and chairman of the Hammonds Bradford Brewery Co. from 1894 until 1912, the year of his death. He took over on the resignation of the previous chairman at a time when the company had paid no dividend for three years. Under Dobson, the firm's fortunes revived. He was also a Conservative councillor and alderman, and cuts a prosperous-looking figure complete with his watch chain.

*Above:* The name of the Yorkshire Divan at Gate Street went back to the Chartist rising of 1848 when it was described as a Chartist beershop and was searched by the police. It is pictured here in the 1920s. Alfred Worsman was licensee in turn of several Bradford pubs. Edgar Wheelwright's signworks is next door. It was eventually granted a full licence in 1961 but was demolished in the general redevelopment of Manchester Road.

*Opposite above:* Another pub that was destroyed in the name of redevelopment was the Horse and Trumpet, located a little further down Manchester Road from the Divan. It had been licensed in 1838 and is seen here as a Ramsden's house, *c.* 1960.

*Opposite below:* The Lister's Arms on a rainy day in 1957. This pub took its name from its owner and builder E.C. Lister, father of Samuel. It opened in 1826 when the new Manchester Road, which provided a straighter route than the winding Bowling Old Lane, was finished. Bought by James Hammond in 1864, it was partly rebuilt and it still stands, although the row of shops just visible on the right have gone.

*Above:* The Bridge Tavern in Bowling Old Lane was part of a typical development of the time, comprising eight houses of which three formed a beerhouse with an internal layout of bar, tap room, parlour and upstairs club room. It was bought by Waller & Son in 1872 and eventually became Tetley's. The eponymous bridge is over the Bowling Beck, which is now no longer visible. The adjoining housing and factory buildings, seen here in the mid-1980s, have all been demolished.

*Opposite above:* The Old Red Ginn in Bowling Old Lane dated back to the early eighteenth century. It was also a farm, but the ginn of its name refers to the device for drawing coal to the surface of a pit, of which there were once several hereabouts.

*Opposite below:* The old pub was demolished in 1968 and replaced by this Tetley's building which, according to the local newspaper, had Swedish-style seating in the public bar. This photograph is from the mid-1980s. Now the blocks of flats no longer tower above it.

Converted to an inn from cottages at the close of the eighteenth century, the best known licensee of the Prince of Wales in Bowling Old Lane was Albert Cowling, whose parents took it in 1874. Albert bought it in 1912 and also carried on a wine and spirit and bottling business there. Edith Crawley was the manageress here for twenty-five years in the 1920s to 1940s and was in charge of the well-known advert: 'Half a pint of ale, a meat pie, a packet of Woodbines and change out of sixpence'. Despite or perhaps because of his job, Albert was a strong believer in temperance and endowed £100 on St Stephen's church for two annual sermons on that theme. He was also a strong Tory and represented them in the council. On his death in 1952, Tetleys bought the Prince of Wales. It is pictured here under their ownership in the mid-1980s.

The Punch Bowl Hotel stood in Park Lane, a substantial public house granted a full licence in 1855. Landlord Thomas Broadley, the captain of the Bradford Football Club, fell foul of increased concern over gambling in 1898 when he was fined for men playing at 'tippit' and raffling a cockerel there. The Punch Bowl Hotel was photographed here in the late 1950s.

Like many others, the Punch Bowl became a Melbourne house. This advertisement for their ales is taken from a Prince's Theatre programme of 1939.

Also in Park Lane, Robert Armstrong got a licence for the hotel he had built in 1854. The Armstrong Hotel had its own brewhouse and a bottling plant for the outdoor family trade. The Ilkley Brewery Co. bought it in 1897. This company was taken over by Hammonds in 1923. It was photographed here in1959

At Bankfoot, the Woodman Inn opened in the 1820s, when the Red Lion opposite was also rebuilt. The landlord Joseph Strutt was also a joiner, hence presumably the name. It was a Stocks' house when it was photographed here in the 1920s.

Benjamin Sugden was the landlord at the Old House at Home in Little Horton Lane from 1866. The pub was appropriately named as it formed part of a house which dated back to 1669. Mr Sugden is at the centre of this photograph with his wife Sarah. Tragically, he hanged himself in May 1901 in an adjoining stable under the pressure of the pain of rheumatic gout which, according to the inquest, kept him from sleeping. On a lighter note, before the council estate was built, whippet racing was popular in the fields behind the pub. The new owners, John Smiths, replaced it in 1966 with a new Old House but this too has now closed.

This beerhouse higher up Little Horton Lane was originally named the Masons Tavern and became the New House at Home after the Old House opened. John Fletcher, who took over in 1920, was the landlord when this photograph was taken.

John Benn was the licensee of the Fox and Pheasant on the other side of Little Horton Lane from the New House at Home from 1894 to 1901, although it is not known if he is one of the three characters pictured here. The Fox and Pheasant has been a public house since 1777 when Joseph Bonnell built it but it was originally known as the Hare and Hounds.

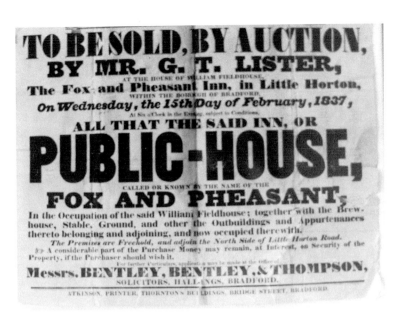

An 1837 auction poster for the Fox and Pheasant. It was sold for £450 to Jonathan Hardy of Low Moor and was later owned by brewers Brear & Brown and afterwards by Ramsdens, and so to Tetleys.

The Fox and Pheasant was modernised in 1959-60 although the original shape is still clearly discernible in this mid-1980s photograph.

Although this is a book about pubs, I must also mention the club. Bradford was noted as a great centre of the club movement with no fewer than 155 listed in a paper published in 1907. These clubs comprised political, trade and working men's clubs, plus friendly societies, Irish, sport and social clubs. Pictured here in around 1900 with some members is the Chapel Green Liberal Club at the end of Thornton Lane, formed sometime in the early 1880s. Such clubs then had a strong political element but games were also important from the start. Before the First World War, Harry Virr played billiards there and was the English champion on several occasions. They were more exclusively male than pubs were and for many years ladies here were only allowed in on election nights and on Christmas Eve. The original club frontage seen here was removed in 1925 for road widening and the creation of the present premises, in which women are now allowed at all times.

six

West

Like Little Horton Lane, Great Horton Road had a number of middle-class residential streets built along its lower sections from the 1840s, many of which still remain along its eastern side, like Claremont, for example, where the composer Delius was born into a German merchant family. Across what at that time were fields, the road reached the village of Great Horton, which had a little cluster of public houses: the King's Arms, the George and Dragon, the Four Ashes, the Fleece and the Bull's Head. Higher up the hill were two more old inns, the Crown and the Hare and Hounds. Further east from Great Horton Road, Listerhills was developed as a more working-class district with some of its terraced streets named after nineteenth-century notables like Cobden, Bright and Villiers. It merges into Legrams Lane on its route to Lidget Green.

Thornton Road, passing through industrial and working-class districts, once had three breweries. First was the Old Brewery, Whitaker & Co. which dated back to 1757 and which was on the site where the New Victoria cinema was later built. Later, there was the Devonshire Arms brewery of J.&S. Tordoff adjoining the pub of that name, which merged with Heys in 1919. Finally, there was the Brown Royd brewery of Joseph Spink & Sons, a company which Heys also took over in 1923. The company was long remembered by the bar of that name underneath the Wool Exchange. Thornton Road then passes through Girlington and Four Lane Ends, where both communities were well supplied with pubs, including substantial houses like the Girlington or the Craven Heifer.

From Girlington, you can make your way towards Manningham and the dominating structure of Lister's colossal mills. You meet Whetley Hill into which White Abbey Road merges. There were once two very old pubs here, the Lower and Upper Globes. Along with a number of other properties in this area, including a working-men's club, they were the target of rioters in 2001. The Lower Globe, which was already derelict, was demolished, but the older of the two, the Upper Globe, was still standing the last time I passed, although it too is closed. Though chiefly a nineteenth-century building, the Upper Globe retains some features from the early eighteenth century, and there was probably an inn on this site even earlier. The parish churchyard once contained the grave of landlord William Powell who died in 1770. It bore the inscription:
'Rest, solemn dust, involved in Nature's robe,
Whilst thy poor soul may find a happier globe'

This pub in Great Horton Road was originally a beerhouse licensed as the Shepherd's Inn in 1851. It was renamed the Bentley Arms by landlord William Bentley who was the licensee there from 1864 to 1872. John Reeday took it in 1914 when it was a Holmes' house and thus it passed to Hammonds in 1919.

Bearing the date 1739 and the letters GB for its builder Gilbert Brooksbank, this inn at Great
Horton may lay claim to being the oldest surviving public house in the city. It was described as such
when it was bought by the brewers Stocks in 1889. James Hiley, the licensee when this photograph
was taken, had been there since 1908.

Another old Great Horton inn dating back to the beginning of the nineteenth century is the George and Dragon, photographed about a century later. It had been bought by Bentley's Yorkshire Breweries in 1875. Note the painted signboard. These are always assumed to be typical pub features but in Bradford at least, as this book demonstrates, they were comparatively unusual; it was much more common to simply display the name and that of the brewer.

*Above:* A typical, basic back-street beerhouse of the early 1850s with minimal pub features, the West End Tavern was in Morpeth Street in Listerhills. Beer was at first brewed on the premises but like most others, it was later supplied by a brewery and tied to one in particular, in this instance to J.R. Holmes and so to Hammonds. It closed in 1924 not long after this photograph was taken; its licence was one of those compensated under the 1904 scheme. The money was distributed in a typical split: £2,635 to the brewery and £365 to the tenant. Three other pubs in the area, the Tumbling Hill Tavern, the Milton Arms and the Gardeners Arms in Melville Street, all closed that year.

*Opposite above:* The Fire Brigade in Southfield Lane opened in 1867, after a conversion from three houses and a shop. Shortly after its opening, it was bought by Joseph Hardy and John Schofield Briggs, who ran the Albion Brewery in Low Lane in Clayton, one of a number of small breweries once working in the district. It was sold to Wallers in 1924, along with the Albion at Clayton, and hence ultimately to Tetleys.

*Opposite below:* There had been an earlier Bull's Head Inn at Great Horton but this one at Paternoster Lane was a beerhouse granted a full licence in 1868. It was a Stocks' house when photographed here in the 1920s.

*Above:* The photograph of the Preston Hotel in Preston Place was taken in the early 1920s when it was a Stocks' house. It had been established as a street corner beerhouse in 1868 and might have been expected to go the way of so many others but it survived and in 1983 became the Fighting Cock, a real ale pub.

*Opposite above:* Another early 1920s photograph of a Stocks' house, this is the Second West Hotel at Lidget Green, a mid-1850s public house which originally had its own brewhouse and stabling and adjoining butcher's shop. It was named after the regiment – the Second West Yorkshire.

*Opposite below:* The Red Lion at Four Lane Ends was opened in 1865 by Abraham Settle, who initially named it after himself. Fully licensed from 1875, it was later a J.R. Holmes' pub and thus went to Hammonds in 1919, around when this photograph was taken. The brewers Samuel Smith bought it in 1976.

The Girlington Concertina Band demonstrates the thriving musical life of pubs outside the Shoulder of Mutton in Thornton Road sometime before the First World War. Seated next to the drum is Joseph Coe minus his concertina – he had pawned it that morning. Sale particulars of 1898 refer to the first floor club room with music licence where no doubt the band rehearsed. John Henry Dewhirst, the first landlord and owner in 1868, was also a butcher, hence its name.

The public house the Lower Globe in Whetley Hill dated back to the beginning of the nineteenth century in older property. When it was photographed here, it was owned and run by John Jackson with his wife Ellen who had been there since 1888. After his death in 1913, she followed a well-worn Bradford path to Morecambe and the pub was sold to the brewers John Smiths. The adjoining old cottages were later demolished and the pub was eventually derelict for some time before being set alight by rioters in 2001 in a sad end for such a historic property.

*Above:* Our last pub was technically beyond the Bradford borough boundary until 1882 when Heaton was incorporated within it. The Fountain Inn, at the corner of Syke Road and Heaton Road, was built by William Sugden in 1856 in a typical development. Heys bought it in 1897 and it is seen here sometime in the 1920s. When I used to drink here in the early 1970s, it retained the old-fashioned interior; this was altered in the mid-1980s. The cottages to the left now form part of the pub car park.

*Opposite above:* The Lilycroft Hotel at the junction of Lilycroft Road and Beamsley Street in the early 1960s. The massive chimney of Lister's mills is visible above it. An inventory of 1927 showed it as having a smoke room, bar parlour, filling bar and vaults, the latter having various sets of dominoes, draughts and a mahogany shove halfpenny board, plus earthen and pewter spittoons. The Lilycroft was replaced by new premises in 1967 when the older housing here was cleared.

*Opposite below:* One must not forget the other essential element of the drinking scene, the off-licence. Created for beer by statute in 1834, they became common in the nineteenth century. This 1920s photograph depicts the one at the junction of Oak Lane and Victor Street, below Lister's Mill. This side of that street was subsequently demolished.

# Other local titles published by The History Press

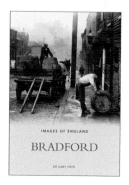

## Bradford
Dr Gary Firth

This selection of more than 200 old photographs recalls Bradford during the period of over half a century from 1880 to the 1950s. The images recall buildings and streets long gone as well as stir memories of the way of life of men, women and children going about their work and play in this busy, vibrant manufacturing city.

0 7524 3019 X

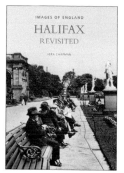

## Halifax Revisited
Vera Chapman

Halifax is characterised by steep slopes and deep valleys, sett-paved streets and nearby moorland. It has an industrial past of woollen mills, canals and railways, the wharves and stations of which liberally dot the countryside. The town today reflects the changes wrought by the Victorians, who created broad streets and fine buildings. This collection of over 200 archive images illustrates the history of Halifax as it once was and records how the town has developed since the mid-eighteenth century.

0 7524 3047 5

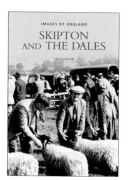

## Skipton and the Dales
Ken Ellwood

Illustrated with over 200 archive images, this volume presents a memorable account of Skipton and its surrounding villages. They include views of schools, buildings, businesses and local characters as well as aerial photographs of this part of the Dales. Special attention is also paid to the airmen from the villages around Skipton who lost their lives in the Second World War.

0 7524 3058 0

## Yorkshire County Cricket Club: 100 Greats
Mick Pope and Paul Dyson

This book features 100 of the cricketers who have shaped Yorkshire CCC; from George Anderson, who first played for Yorkshire in 1850 – before the official club was constituted – through to Matthew Hoggard, who received the coveted county cap in 2000. Between these pages is a glimpse of their characters – which are often colourful, sometimes controversial and invariably commanding – portrayed through short biographies, each of which is accompanied by a photograph and statistical profile.

0 7524 2179 4

If you are interested in purchasing other books published by The History Press, or in case you have difficulty finding any of our books in your local bookshop, you can also place orders directly through our website
www.thehistorypress.co.uk